Contents

Alfred Music
P.O. Box 10003
Van Nuys, CA 91410-0003
alfred.com

ISBN-10: 0-7579-9096-7
ISBN-13: 978-0-7579-9096-0

Piano Image Courtesy of Yamaha Corporation

From the M-G-M Motion Picture "GREEN DOLPHIN STREET"

ON GREEN DOLPHIN STREET

Words by
NED WASHINGTON

Music by
BRONISLAU KAPER
Arranged by ROBERT SCHULTZ

On Green Dolphin Street - 3 - 1
AFM01028
AS006

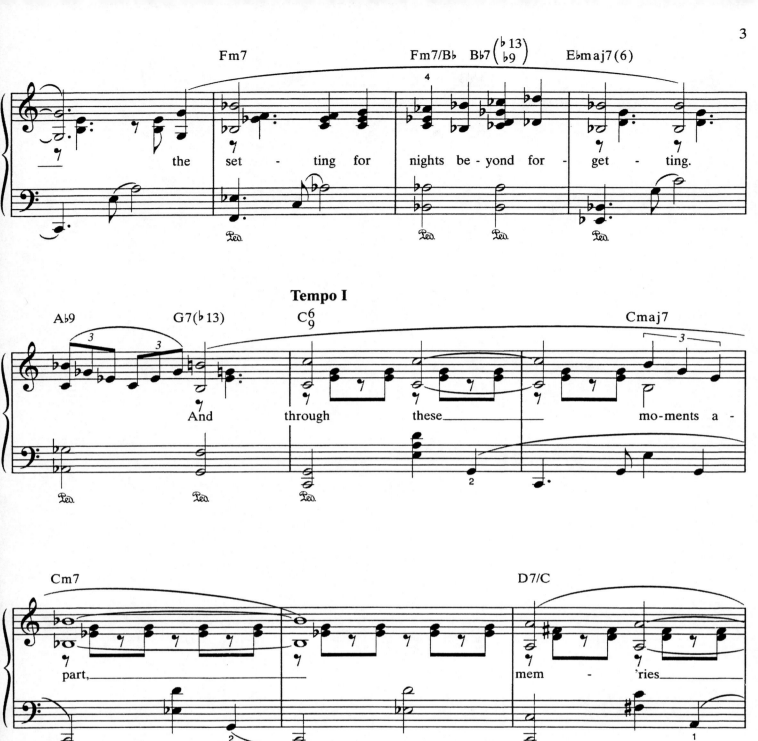

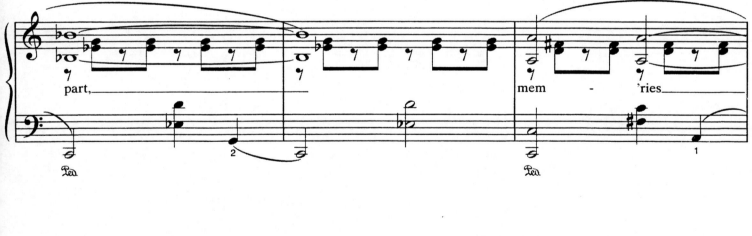

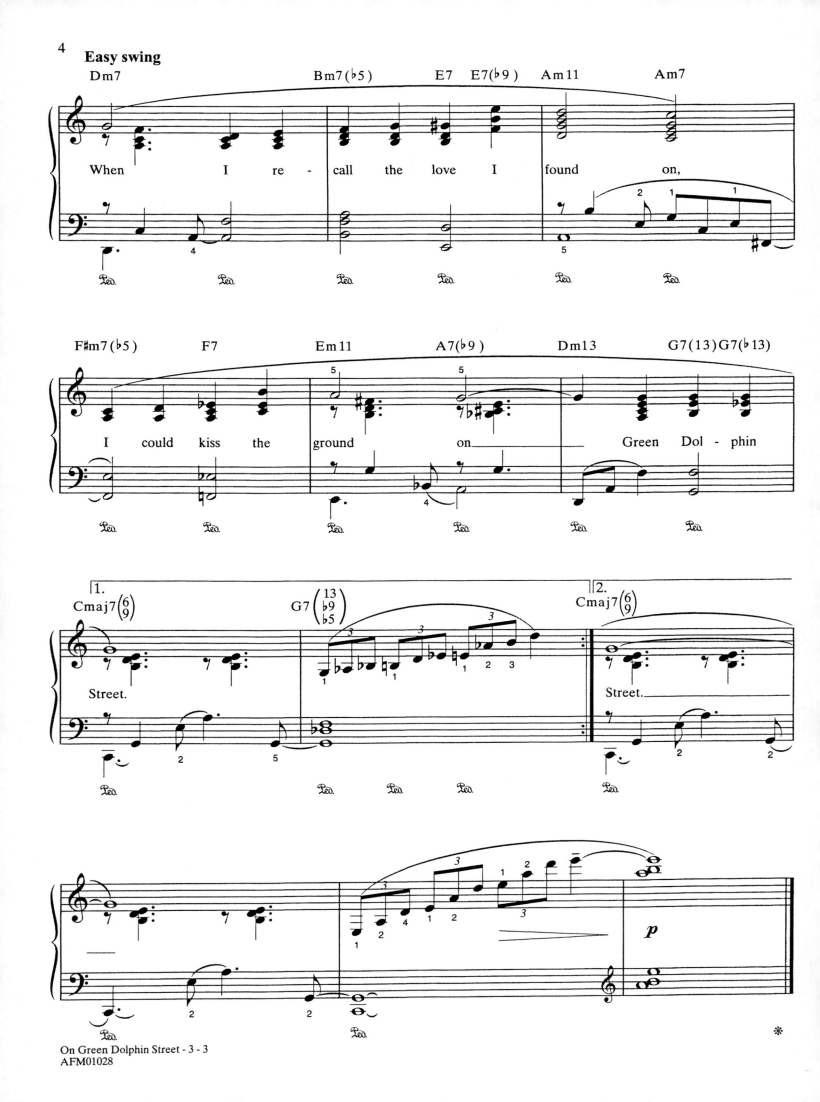

On Green Dolphin Street - 3 - 3
AFM01028

EVERYTIME WE SAY GOODBYE

Words and Music by
COLE PORTER
Arranged by ROBERT SCHULTZ

Everytime We Say Goodbye - 3 - 1
AFM01028
AS006

From the Broadway Musical "Oh, Kay!"

SOMEONE TO WATCH OVER ME

Words and Music by
GEORGE GERSHWIN and IRA GERSHWIN
Arranged by ROBERT SCHULTZ

LOVER MAN
(Oh, Where Can You Be?)

Words and Music by JIMMY DAVIS,
ROGER "RAM" RAMIREZ and JIMMY SHERMAN
Arranged by ROBERT SCHULTZ

MORE THAN YOU KNOW

Words by
WILLIAM ROSE and EDWARD ELISCU

Music by
VINCENT YOUMANS
Arranged by ROBERT SCHULTZ

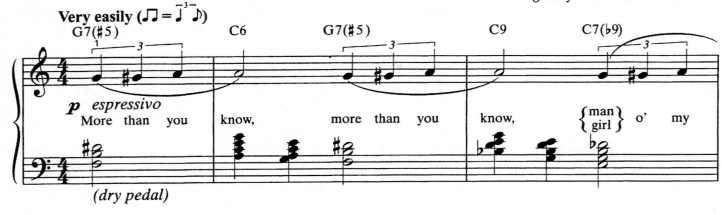

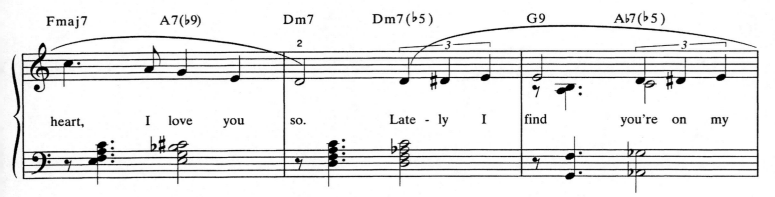

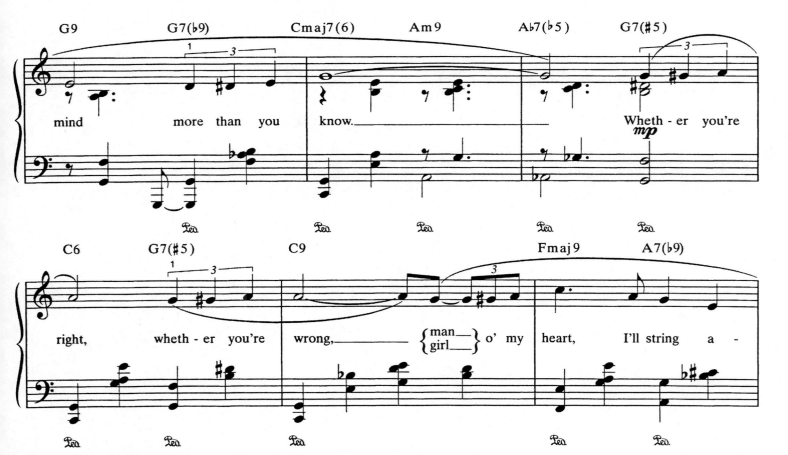

More Than You Know - 3 - 1
AFM01028
AS006

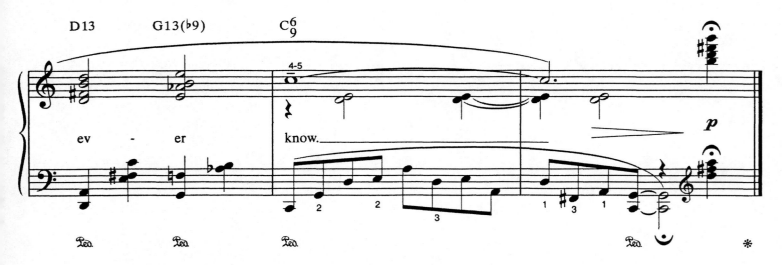

SKYLARK

Lyrics by
JOHNNY MERCER

Music by
HOAGY CARMICHAEL
Arranged by ROBERT SCHULTZ

MY FOOLISH HEART

Words by
NED WASHINGTON

Music by
VICTOR YOUNG
Arranged by ROBERT SCHULTZ

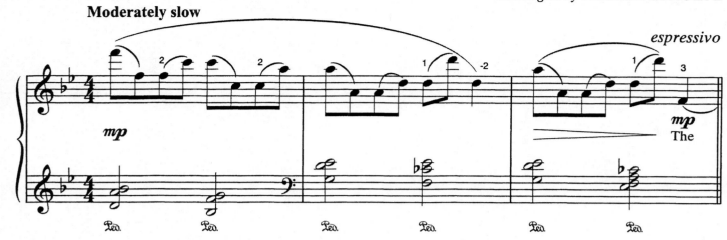

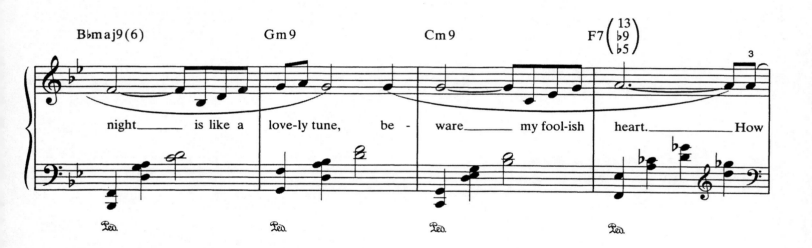

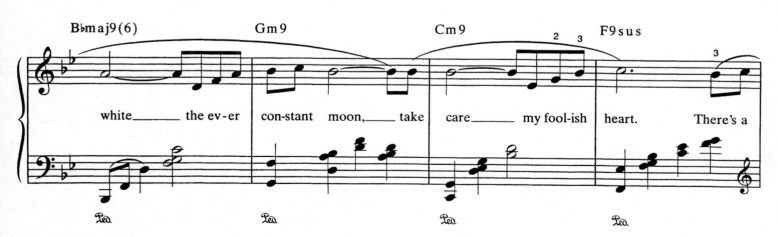

My Foolish Heart - 3 - 1
AFM01028
AS006

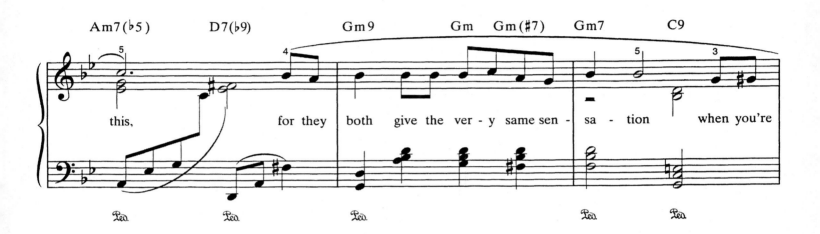

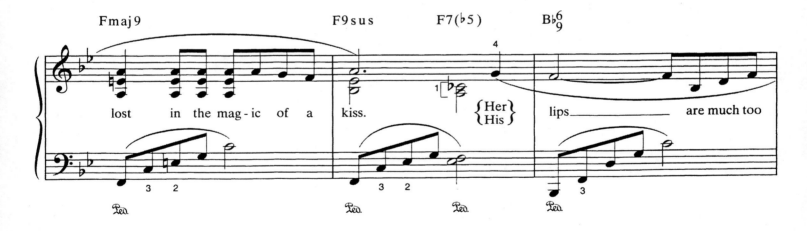

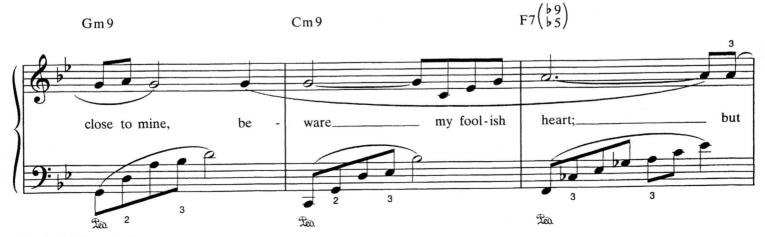

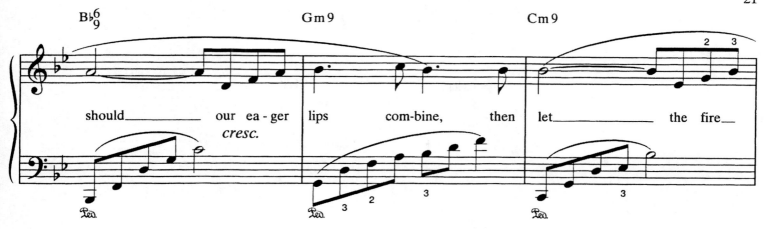

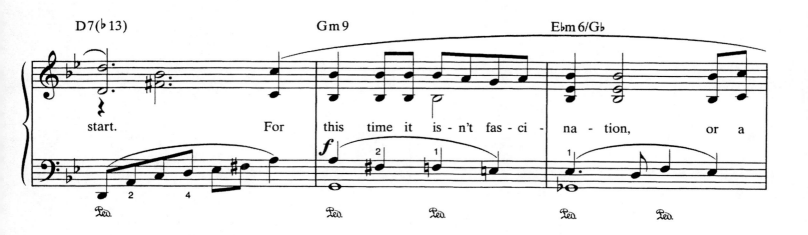

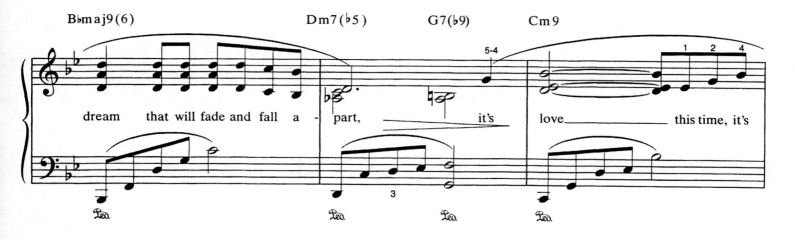

My Foolish Heart - 3 - 3
AFM01028

GROOVIN' HIGH

By JOHN "DIZZY" GILLESPIE
Arranged by ROBERT SCHULTZ

Groovin' High - 2 - 1
AFM01028
AS006

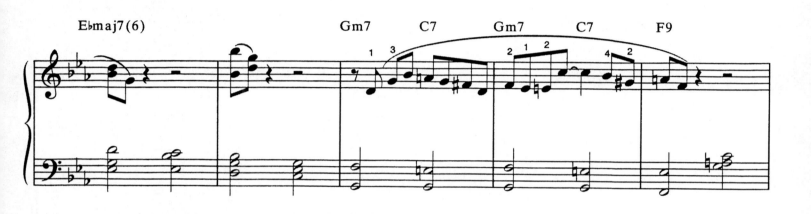

JUST FRIENDS

Words by
SAM M. LEWIS

Music by
JOHN KLENNER
Arranged by ROBERT SCHULTZ

Just Friends - 2 - 1
AFM01028
AS006

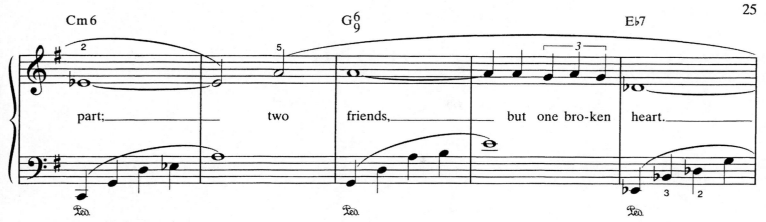

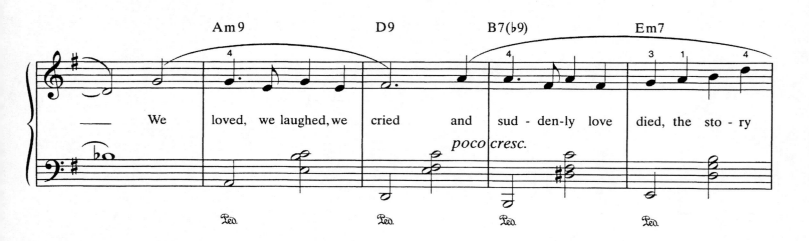

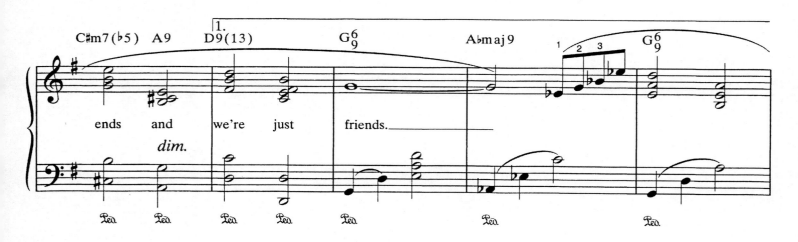

From the Metro-Goldwyn-Mayer Motion Picture "SHOOT THE MOON"
Sugar Babies

DON'T BLAME ME

Words by
DOROTHY FIELDS

Music by
JIMMY McHUGH
Arranged by ROBERT SCHULTZ

From the Twentieth Century-Fox Technicolor Musical "BILLY ROSE'S DIAMOND HORSESHOE"

THE MORE I SEE YOU

Words by
MACK GORDON

Music by
HARRY WARREN
Arranged by ROBERT SCHULTZ

TIME AFTER TIME

Words by
SAMMY CAHN

Music by
JULE STYNE
Arranged by ROBERT SCHULTZ

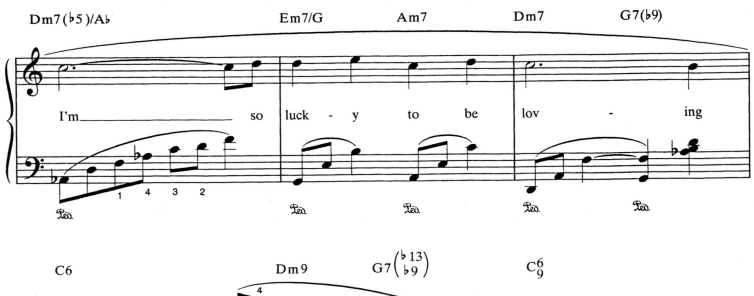

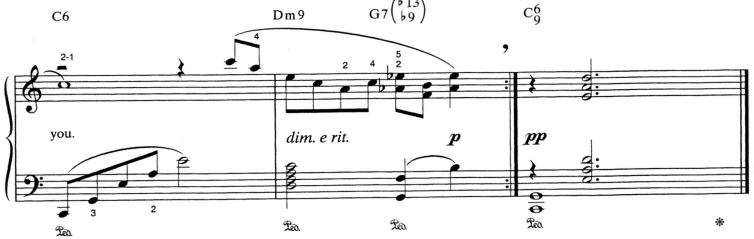

MOONLIGHT IN VERMONT

Words by
JOHN BLACKBURN

Music by
KARL SUESSDORF
Arranged by ROBERT SCHULTZ

Moonlight in Vermont - 3 - 1
AFM01028
AS006

ROBERT SCHULTZ

With more than three thousand piano arrangements, transcriptions, and original works in print, ROBERT SCHULTZ is one of America's most published and prolific writers. Schultz joined the arranging staff at Columbia Pictures Publications in 1979 which became Warner Bros. Publications and is now Alfred Music. He held the position of senior keyboard editor from 1980 to 1989. Although Schultz focuses primarily on piano writing, his output also includes original orchestral works, chamber music, works for solo instruments, vocal music, and incidental music for several plays. Recordings of Schultz's original piano compositions and transcriptions have been released on the ACA Digital label. Outstanding reviews in *The American Music Teacher, Clavier,* and *Piano Quarterly* reflect the enthusiasm with which his piano works have been received. In-depth information about Robert Schultz and *The Schultz Piano Library* is available at the Web site: www.schultzmusic.com.